MW00465217

Be Still Moments

A Collection of Writings and Devotionals

Be Still Moments

A Collection of Writings and Devotionals

© 2010 Joanne E. Sampl
Foreword by Margaret Cook

ALL SHE WRIT PUBLISHING

Be Still Moments
A Collection of Writings and Devotionals

Requests for information should be addressed to:
All She Writ Publishing, P.O. Box 1193,
Maryland Heights, MO 63043-0193

ISBN-13: 978-0615572444

Published for the benefit of Next-Step-of-Faith.com ministry.

Interior design by Jill Seidelman
Proofreading assistance by Charlotte W. O'Brien
Printed in the United States of America.
Published in affiliation with Create Space.

Acknowledgements

Above all, Joanne would acknowledge the inspiration and gifts of God that made all things possible in her life, including these creative works.

This book is a compilation of writings that Joanne Sampl planned to share. She started a ministry to encourage Christians to write about their faith experiences, and she lead by example. She took time in her busy life to write about her experiences, and she planned to publish a book someday. In her memory, we fulfill that plan by publishing her work after the completion of her life. Joanne also left a document that described how much people that shared her life shaped her faith journey. No words could express how much that was true about her family. Joanne's joy and energy reflected God's love in her love for her husband, Michael Sampl, her sons Eric and Adam Spaeth, Michael's children Diana and Mike, Jr. Mike, Jr.'s children Shaun and Alexis blessed Joanne with the joys of grandmothering.

The list of people Joanne mentioned in one of her notes was admittedly a partial list. She titled the list a "Catalog of Connections." She wanted to particularly thank and embrace the people who made such a difference in her life and encouraged her in her creativity and faith. With prayer, we recognize all of the people that God brought into Joanne's life and all of the people with whom she had the joy of sharing her gifts. The partial (alphabetized) list is Joanne's way of acknowledging the precious friendships she enjoyed.

Catalog of Connections (May 16, 2007)

So, with the deepest clearest understanding that my very best friend is my Michael, I am listing in my head all the real friends I have now. I ache that there are so many of them that I made long promises of "we'll get together when…" and won't be able to fulfill those promises.

LORD, you fulfill them for me. You've always been the best part of these friendships, because they are and always have been about knowing you, sharing you, and growing closer to you.

So, here is my Catalog of Connections – Spiritual Sisters and Deep Faith Friends who I am already aching that I won't get to share their day to days with someday.

Bonnie Schulte	Ginny Gilbertsen	Pamela Popp
Cindy Amelung	Pastor Keith Gillming	Melanie Priest
Shannon Ayers	Karla Goldhamme	Rhonda Rhea
Lana Ladd Baker	Betty Herin	Richie Rhea
Denise Basler	Yvonne Hilbert	Lisa Boalt Richardson
Emily Basler	Toni Hiles	Ruth Rodemich
Heather Baur	Carol Ilbery	Jan Root
Anne Berger	Della Johnson	Peanuts Rudolph
Ray Bombardieri	Tina Johnson	Rhonda Ruester
Holly Brand	Marilyn Jones	Travina Saindon
Janet Bridgeforth	Dr. Karen Kalinevitch	Julie Sanders
Kelly Campbell	Denise Kiehl	Chris Sasse
Lucy Carr	Sandy Knight	Susanne Scheppmann
Beth Caster	Cindy Layman	Sherrill Schlimpert
Kevin Cawley	Christine Lewis	Vickie Silkey
Sandy Crane	Rita Lindner	Kim Spaan
Kathy D'Amico	Cheryl Linn	Carla Standley
Lorre Daniels	Karen Matteson	Len Steber
Brian Dent	Sheila McMichael	Cindy Taylor
Daniel & Laura Duke	Jennifer Miller	Pam Teson
Sharon Dunn	Regina Murphy	Donna Thielker
Pam Faygal	Sr. Jo Nemec	Ruth Thompson
Karen Fields	Monica Notz	Carol Villalobos
Dana Frese	Angie Olmsted	Laura Wells
Ken Fuller	Charlotte Petty	Sheila Whittington
Nancy Funke	Kim Pitman	Jan Wilson

Foreword

Joanne has a journal entry from May 10, 2007. She wrote, "I dared to dream a few years ago, Lord, that I would have a ministry of hope, healing and help for people who need your comfort. You let me learn quickly how to design websites and put into place my marketing and business senses to help churches and businesses."

While Joanne was preparing to live that dream, she took classes, entered writing contests and honed her writing skills. She helped many businesses and churches start, grow and succeed. She loved being creative and helpful. If a life would be touched or changed through anything, she was willing to try it.

Joanne founded a website to encourage women to write about their faith experiences. She was open-hearted about accepting submissions and she did not "edit." She mentored writers, spoke to groups and encouraged writing as a spiritual practice.

I enjoyed hearing her ideas and reading her writing. Soon after she founded the Next Step of Faith website (www.Next-Step-of-Faith.com), Joanne asked me to write a monthly column to encourage writers. I was glad to help and we had many laughs working together.

When Joanne found out she had cancer, she asked me to "take over" the tasks for the Next Step of Faith. We had no idea how swiftly she would courageously face that illness. We prayed for healing, and we asked every question of faith that anyone would ask when someone young and vibrant encounters something so difficult. Through it all, Joanne's faith kept growing. I spent Sunday afternoons with her at first and helped with the proofreading, posting and finding the scripture verses.

In those precious Sunday worship experiences, Joanne talked about her vision for telling the stories of women and the ways God speaks to them and through them. She hoped to publish an annual book with the best submissions of the year. She was going to form a publishing company to help writers who were struggling to get books published, and she wanted to help more authors have effective websites and marketing.

Joanne planned to publish a collection called <u>Be Still Moments</u>. At the end of 2010, her husband Michael compiled the first edition for friends and family. In the spirit of her vision, I humbly pick up the mantle and publish this selection of Joanne's writing. I have updated this second edition and made some revisions.

Joanne's writing is essentially unedited. I appreciate the help of friends who helped with proofreading and error correction. The sale proceeds will support the ongoing Next Step of Faith ministry in memory of Joanne Sampl.

May God bless you and encourage you as you grow in faith and get to know Joanne in these pages. Many sorely miss her warmth and humor, but her words of hope and encouragement remind us that she lives forevermore.

In Christ,

Margaret Cook
Sister, Sister in Christ, Next Step of Faith collaborator/writing coach, Next Step Up Communication Summer Intern, etc.

"And we know that in all things God works for the good of those who love him, who have been called according to his purpose."
– Romans 8:28

Contents

Be Still Moments

A Collection of Writings and Devotionals

Open a Box of Childhood

I have a small yearning that overwhelms me every fall. Okay, it can get to be a pretty big yearning for me. Now, just so you know, I'm not one to spend a lot of time in the malls or shopping for clothes. Personally, I'd rather spend an afternoon in the hardware store, checking out the latest hardware gadgets that make a house more up-to-date without spending a lot of money. But my yearning does involve shopping.

When the last few weeks of summer start up, I start stock piling the object of my yearning: school supplies. It's a sickness really. I can lose at least an hour sorting through all the different kinds of pens available every school year. And I used to buy packets and packets of loose-leaf paper, just because fall was the cheapest time of year to buy them. As much as my children hated all those handwritten exercises and homework, I loved to see my well-preserved school supply box get used. For years, it seemed that I spent almost as much on pens, folders, binders, highlighters, crayons, markers and scissors as I did on back-to-school clothes for both my boys. They may have needed new jeans, but I always made sure they had enough items in the school supply box to get their homework done.

When my sons were both in high school, I was forced to redirect my school supply spending to more important things - like track shoes and activity passes. They didn't need my loose-leaf packets of paper anymore. They were, however, going through lots of copier paper and inkjet cartridges. Times were changing, their needs were changing, and my school supply box sat dormant with hardening crayons and drying markers.

This year was the saddest fall of all for me. I had nothing to buy for my school supply box. Although one son is still in college and the other one is in the military, neither of them needed me to provide their school supplies. They were old enough to take care of their needs themselves.

I peered into the overcrowded back-to-school aisle at Wal-Mart, watching mothers and children gather long lists of supplies for the start of the school year. I had no reason to fight them for my space in the aisle so I could make the perfect pen selection for the season. I mourned the loss of my overflowing shopping cart. Today, I just needed some shampoo, trash bags, and light bulbs. I didn't need any school supplies - for anyone.

It was then I decided to start a new box.

I haven't spent enough time lately remembering what beautiful and special children God gave me. I work full time now. My stay-at-home mom days are over. My sons are grown men now. But, they were such adorable boys. I called them my sunshines, and I sang to them every morning and read to them nearly every night. We had designated positions for cuddling on the sofa while we watched TV. We threw the baseball mitts on the top shelf of the front closet for those quick games of catch we'd play after school.

So now, instead of filling a box of school supplies that get used up or dry out, I've started both of my boys' boxes of something different: my memories of their childhood.

And, yes, I have a few pages of their handwritten homework - on loose-leaf paper, of course.

Joanne

Wednesday, September 3, 2008

2

Chaos with a Capital "K"

It's easy to get wrapped up in the hustle and bustle of the season. My "to-do" list seems only shortened by the number of items I've missed. For every item I do scratch off the list by accomplishment or expiration, I replace with two or three more items. Every waking hour seems to be like a never-ending ping-pong match in my head. One thought bounces to another thought, then that thought spirals back to another. I'm even finding my hours when I am asleep are almost as chaotic as my hours awake. My dreams seem to be my subconscious reminding me to add things to my list: gift ideas, activities, more gift ideas, Christmas cards, business meetings, phone calls, more gift ideas, time with treasured friends, groceries, budgeting, work projects, goals for next year, more gift ideas, church meetings and events, memories of loved ones, sched-ules, traditions, more gift ideas, etc. Day and night, I seem to be bombarded with chaos.

Somewhere there is peace - *The King of Peace.*

It's now that I remember my King. Was He even on my list? Where was He in my chaotic thoughts and plans: First? Last? No where? Where is He in my day or night: First? Last? Some where in between? Not at all? Will Christmas still turn over on the calendar if I don't get that card written or that gift bought? Yes. Will we starve if I wait an hour to start grocery shopping? No. Will the chaos stop if I put my King first? No. Will I have peace through my chaos? Yes.

"But seek first his kingdom and his righteousness, and all these things will be given to you as well..

– Matthew 6:33

Did I first seek His Kingdom in my life? All my needs and maybe a few of my wants on my list are met by God when He's the King of my day, my night, my hour, my list.

So, it's just a few more days until Christmas. When I realize my ping-pong thoughts have bounced me away from peace again, it's time to spell the chaos in my life with a capital "K" – for my *King of Peace*.

This I Pray...

Lord, you are my God. You have given order to all of creation. Give me your order to my priorities for this day. But let it begin with your reign in my heart. Let me center on your peace for me, not my desires for myself.

Joanne

December 2007

Why Does God Allow Sad Stories?

A hopeful romantic – that's how I describe myself. In my imagination, the boy always gets the girl and they ride off together into the sunset. In my imagination, the two marry in the most spectacular ceremony of the century. Soon, they become parents of ideal, healthy children who respect and honor their parents and grow up into courageous astronauts, doctors and Noble Peace Prize winners. In my imagination, there is always a happy ending.

So, why isn't God a hopeful romantic like me? Why doesn't He smooth out the rough spots of our lives and create a utopia for us? Why do sweet, dear, wonderful people have to suffer for months and years with circumstances that completely overwhelm them?

I am blessed to have some really good friends who share their hearts and burdens with me. I pray for them faithfully. They each have some circumstance that seems insurmountable. One friend has a serious health issue and has seen doctors and specialists for over twenty years. No one can diagnose her problem, let alone offer some hope or cure. Another friend has a child with health and psychological complications requiring even more attention and energy than she has to give. Another friend is battling the corporate pressure of intensely high expectations and manipulative personal criticisms, but just recently was fired by a plot of corporate sabotage. She debates going back into the harsh work environment, but with no savings and living alone, she has little choice. Another friend is committed to her marriage, although the loneliness and dysfunctions have reeked out any joy and emotional connection for her in the relationship.

These are just a few stories of the women around me who are asking the question, "Why does God allow this in my life?"

There is no easy answer. Each one of these friends is in a battle for her faith and her hope. Each one is on the verge of quitting, of allowing her hopeful romantic story to end bitterly, of allowing a part of herself to die in the process of just surviving instead of conquering. Each one is feeling that God isn't hearing her prayers let alone answering them. Each one is pouring out everything she has to make it one more week, one more day, and sometimes one more hour.

I ache for each one of them and join them in their burden as much as I can.

There is a part of me that wants to uphold the character of God to them right now. "God isn't doing this to you," I told one friend going through a battle with her middle child.

She snapped back with, "But He is allowing it." I couldn't argue with her point. I couldn't argue with the pain in her voice or the sense of betrayal and frustration she was feeling. She was exhausted. She just needed one hopeful, romantic storybook ending for the situation so she could go on for one more week, one more day, one more hour.

None of my spiritual disciplines or "have you tried" list of suggestions would comfort her. All I could ask was how she was doing in her personal bible study. I was pleased with her answer. It was the first bright spot of the conversation. "It's great!" She shared. "I'm loving it."

Then, I realized she was reading the only perpetually hopeful, romantic story there is: The Story of God. Overwhelming circumstances are part of this world since the first sin in the Garden of Eden. People of every walk of life on this planet have faced life and death, famine and starvation, disease and perversion of every kind. We are not alone in being overwhelmed by our circumstances.

In fact, in so many ways, our modern conveniences have even reduced the degree of intensity of our circumstances. We have trained doctors and researchers trying to help find cures and treatments for medical conditions that never even had a diagnosis a hundred years ago. We have telephones, computers, e-mail and the internet to share our burdens through, instead of being so isolated and alone without technology that we could literally die without anyone knowing or caring.

My husband and I used to joke about how I would never make it if I lived in another time period or in another culture. Indoor plumbing is an absolute must for me. Microwaves and coffee makers are a close second. Adjustable thermostats with whole house air conditioning and heating are mandatory for me.

I could live without my computer or cell phone, but I wouldn't survive without my minivan to zip over to a friend's house for tea or a chat.

So, why does God allow circumstances that overwhelm us? Why does He allow sadness, death and devastation to be part of this world? He can move a mountain, change a heart, heal the sick, and raise the dead if He wanted to, right? Why aren't we protected from the evil one, the perverse sin and the fear of a hopeless future?

"God has not promised to protect us completely from the evil in the world," Diane Langberg, Ph.D. writes in her book On the Threshold of Hope for survivors of sexual abuse. "What He will do is anything and everything to preserve you in Christ. He will protect the life of God in you. He is your refuge from anything that would take you away from God." (Langberg 1999, 211)

So, my prayer for you, my dear friends, is that you sense that the hopeful, romantic story is still happening in your lives. God has His arms securely around you, His Spirit is unquestionably in you, and His Light is shining in your eyes. You and Jesus are the hopeful, romantic story of oneness. He's the boy. You're the girl. He's the groom. You're the bride. The day you accepted Him as your Lord and Savior was the most spectacular ceremony of all time. Your union with Him has created life and affected all of creation. Your name is written in His book. He wrote love letter after love letter to you in the Scriptures. He's put you in a time of history that you can connect to more people, be more productive with your time and resources, and really accelerate your opportunities to heal, to grow and to talk about your hopeful romantic story of God with others.

And, because you are in a marriage with Jesus, I hope and pray you feel His tears and His burden for what you are going through. Jesus loves you. He's groaning with you. He's sharing your burden.

Recently, I heard a pastor describe God's heart for us when we are going through devastations like Hurricane Katrina. He said it so simply, "An act of God is also the tears of God."

In your lives, in your situation and in your overwhelming circumstances, God is still writing the most hopeful, romantic, and "happily-ever-after for eternity" story in you. You are not alone. Your Groom is with you. How I pray you let Him comfort you through your bible study, your prayer life and your circumstances.

"I have loved you with an everlasting love; I have drawn you with loving-kindness."
– Jeremiah 31:3

"Though the mountains be shaken and the hills be removed, yet my unfailing love for you will not be shaken nor my covenant of peace be removed," says the LORD, who has compassion on you.
– Isaiah 54:10

Joanne
October 5, 2005

Fluff with a Deluxe Bath Towel

The consequence of not finishing the laundry can sometimes be the privilege of using the last clean towel in the linen cabinet. I recently became aware of my incomplete task one morning while dashing to the shower. From the far-reaching depths of the untidy closet came a relic of the past. It was once a gorgeous, thick, bright pink bath towel. It was one of four given to me as a wedding present almost fifteen years ago. Somehow, this one escaped the tattering of teenagers and pool parties. It was only slightly faded from the hundreds of washings it had endured through the years.

I felt like a princess as I wrapped up in it. Yes, it was still warm and soft. It wasn't as big as I remembered, but I prefer not to focus on my own size differences of fifteen years gone by either. The label still boldly pronounced its value: *Deluxe.*

As I placed the damp towel on the rack, my mind splashed with the real value of that gift. It was given to me by a dear friend who was a single mother at the same time I was. I knew she didn't have as much money as she had expenses, but she was so excited and happy for me that I was marrying a Christian man, she wanted to buy me something nice. She knew that my "bargain basement" side would always over power my "your worth it" side to go out and buy myself anything as nice as these towels. I treasured her sacrificial gift then, and even more so now. I haven't heard from her in over ten years.

Proverbs 18:16 says, *"A gift opens the way for the giver and ushers him into the presence of the great."* Just digging out that old, wonderful towel given to me with joy and love so many years ago still opens my heart towards my distant friend.

I wonder how she is. I wonder where she is. But, most importantly, I wonder if she received as much of a blessing giving these "deluxe" bath towels with such sacrifice and love. I wonder where God has taken her to continue her faith journey with Him.

While we celebrate Easter and think about the Gift Jesus gave us on the Cross, I am so curious about the "Presence of the Great" that Jesus experienced. To be in the Father's presence again after being away for so long must have been an incredible reunion. And because of the Resurrection of Easter, I can hardly wait for my own turn to be wrapped up in the arms of my Savior someday – feeling like a princess – without the fluff but with all the love!

Joanne

April 3, 2007

Gathering the Bundles of Friendship

There are predictable seasons for activities. As soon as the crispness of an autumn breeze jackets me, I start thinking about family traditions, like picking apples and jumping into freshly raked leaves with my kids. Turtlenecks and plaid cotton shirts are pulled out of the closet, and the hunt for thick, warm socks begins. What coat needs to go to the cleaners and which one is it time to replace become serious decisions.

And then, like clockwork, I start the emotional bundling of friendships as if I am gathering firewood for the long winter ahead. Whom haven't I talked with lately? Whom did I want to get together with over the summer and just ran out of time? Who is so important to me that I want to make sure they know I care and want to keep the relationship warm and cozy for us both? This list is longer than I expect, but I am grateful to God that each friendship has its own glow of deep, warm memories; honest moments; tender sharing; genuine love and affection. Some have burned longer than others, but each one is vital to the kindling in my heart.

Then the storm of busyness hits and scatters my best intentions. Did her birthday slip away, and I didn't send a card? Has it been three days since she left a voice mail, and I haven't had time to call her back? Has it already been a month since I promised to have lunch with her?

This I Pray...

Lord, help me make order out of the disorder of my life, so the people who really matter to me know how much I care.

In response, the Lord opens a door from heaven of calmness, and the gentle fall breeze returns. The colorful leaves still dance to the ground, but I at least have time to watch. How I choose to spend this calmness is the real decision. As sweet, hot chocolate sips fill my bible study time, the Word nourishes me. Although I ache to spend time with my girlfriends and feel pressure to squeeze time away from my first Priority to meet my needs for connection, I know I must first spend time with my Best Friend.

After all, it was His Gift to me that I should be blessed with such a bundle of friendships.

I read His Letter to me expectantly, discovering new principles out of familiar lines. I snuggle up with His obvious love for me, wrapped up in His personally hand-woven blanket. His warmth for me is a blaze.

One by one, each special friend comes again to my mind. He's gathering them for me in my heart, reminding me of why He made them so special and of how much I have grown because they are part of my life. He warms me with the truths I've seen of His power in their lives.

From some friends, I have learned how to have faith when it seems impossible. How does she keep her faith during serious health issues, or how does another keep faith during unpredictable change? How does she keep her faith when that happened to her?

Or how does she keep her faith when she knows what's still ahead? I have seen the faith the size of a mustard seed actually move mountains in these women's lives.

From other friends, I have learned what hope looks like. How does she smile again after losing her loved one? How does she keep looking ahead to the future when she's had such tragic things in her past? Where does her strength come from when she literally has nothing left? I have watched hope in the Lord not only change lives but actually carry lives on through insurmountable circumstances. The Lord warms me with the flame of hope in their lives when my own hope flickers.

And, then, through the entire bundle of friendships, I am constantly aware of the warmth of genuine love: my love for them, their love for me, but mostly His love for all of us. His are the arms that hold us together, whether for a season or for a lifetime. He holds us to His chest to start the warm glow, and it's His love that spreads through each of us. No wonder I love them so much! It isn't just my love that I feel for them. It is His love added to my love that makes each friendship so warm and inviting.

Jesus is the Gatherer of my bundle of friendships. He holds us together as long as we hold onto Him, so that through each other we will know the warmth of His love more fully, more deeply, more intently. This isn't about whom I have forgotten to call or write, or with whom I've been too busy to stay in touch. This is not about my best intentions, but it is about His best love for us all. My own love will never keep the embers going in these friendships. It is His love through me that really ignites the hearth of friendship.

To all my dear friends who are part of the Lord's fireplace of love in my life, I cherish you all deeply. I have learned so much. I am blessed so much. I am growing so much closer to the Lord because of your love joining in my bundle of friend-ship held by Jesus. Thank you for warming me with your love and His.

"And now these three remain: faith, hope and love. But the greatest of these is love."
– 1 Corinthians 13:13.

Joanne

October 9, 2006

You are "Da Bomb" to God

Where you get your definition needs to be from God's Book.

Dictionaries are useful tools. Words in our vocabulary come alive when they are fully understood. We all assume that Mr. Webster – or whoever wrote your version of the dictionary on your shelf – did his research and defined the words in the dictionary correctly.

So, what about the dictionaries we write in our own lives? Do we do our own research or just assume the meanings of the words said?

A few years ago, I was driving my kids home from school one day and asked my elder son how a presentation went. His answer was a monotone, "It was the bomb." Taking my life dictionary from being raised in the 60s and 70s, I assumed he meant it was a dismal failure. I assumed that he meant it went badly and that he was very discouraged. My reaction was immediately sorrowful.

"Oh, honey, I'm so sorry to hear that." I tried to reassure him, "I'm sure you'll do better next time, honey."

Both my sons looked at me like I was from another planet. We were definitely using different dictionaries.

"No, Mom. It means he did good, really good. The teacher said he was one of the best. He just didn't want you to think he was bragging." His younger brother became my dictionary and explained the definition of his generation to the phrase *"It was the da bomb."*

Then, like a real bomb, both boys exploded in laughter.

So what does God's dictionary say about you? What are the words in His vocabulary for you that come alive because He has defined them so you can understand them?

Colossians 3:12 says we are God's chosen people. Do you know what that means? Do you understand how set apart you are? You are dearly loved by the Creator of the Universe. One of the wisest pastors I ever heard once taught that if we are thinking about ourselves or someone else as anything but a precious child of God, we are wrong. The next time you think of yourself as a bomb where all you see is that you've messed up or failed at something, remember that to God *"You are da bomb!"*

Joanne

July 3, 2006

A Seed of Gratefulness

A town like many others, Sappington teetered on the verge of poverty. The small farming community crusted over with drought and depression. The people of Sappington ached in the loss of their crops, and families huddled around their bare pantries for some hope of prosperity. There was none.

One day, eight-year-old Timmy Johnson stood barefoot in the town square, kicking the dust in the air and watching it catch in the warm summer breeze. His family's farm was one of the hardest hit by the drought. No one heard him whisper a prayer.

"God," he started, "I know you can hear me and see me. The preacher said you can." He looked around to make sure no one else heard him. Timmy's stomach rumbled with hunger pains since there was only enough food for one meal a day.

"So, God, can you answer me one little prayer? Can you fix this? The Bible says if I believe in you, you'll answer my prayers. Please, God! Thank you." Timmy squeezed his eyes shut while he pleaded and thanked the Lord in his prayer.

The heat and lack of food brought Timmy into the shade of the general store porch. He spread his thin body out on the steps of the porch in the shade and quickly fell asleep. His small sleeping body wrestled in the heat, and one of his arms fell between the planking of the porch steps.

Waking an hour later, Timmy felt a cool, round object with his hand under the porch. His eyes strained to see in the darkness what he was touching. It was an apple, a slightly overripe fruit with a softening outer skin and the pungent smell of decay. Timmy brushed the ants off the apple and picked it up.

"Thank you, God," Timmy shouted happily, looking up to the sky. "This is just what we need."

Timmy ran home with the apple and brought it into his house. His mother did not see what Timmy was so excited about. "If it weren't decayed, maybe we could make it into a pie," she said.

Timmy's father was equally unimpressed with his son's find. "Son, it's not worth anything."

Timmy was sure they were wrong.

He carried his treasure out to the barn and cut it open with his pocketknife. He carefully took the seeds from the core, then took a small pot and filled it with dirt and cow manure. He crumbled the remainder of the apple in the dirt, and then buried the seeds a few inches below the top. He trusted God to make an apple tree grow. He sat with his potted seeds under the stars before he went to bed, thanking God for answering his prayer and believing He would keep on answering his prayers.

God was faithful. That night, the tiny town was refreshed by the first gentle rain fall in months. The next night, another gentle rain came while the town's people slept. Timmy spent some time each night sitting beside his potted apple seeds, thanking God for watering the night before. He was so grateful for all God was doing.

Soon, the tiny seeds broke the surface of dirt with small, fragile green sprouts. Timmy was so thrilled to see his patience and his praise to God was working.

One night, Timmy's father came out to him and the pot of apple seeds.

"It looks like you've got something growing, son," the tired farmer said, realizing that his own fields were lifeless. "I'm glad you found those seeds. Maybe someday they'll grow strong apple trees."

"Maybe," Timmy answered quickly. "I just need to thank God everyday."

"I wish I had your faith," his dad said sadly.

"You can, Pa. You just need to be grateful for what you have." Timmy shared again how he found the seeds right after he'd prayed to God, and that he knew God was watching him and knew what he was praying.

"Do you thank God very much, Pa?" Timmy's question was simple and truthful.

"No, son - not very much at all," the father admitted.

"That can change, Pa," Timmy shared. "Thanking God can start as small as a seed, but it can grow every day." Then, the father and son gave God thanks for blessing them with rain and each other.

The next day, tiny green sprouts began to push through the softening soil in the farmer's field.

A seed of gratefulness has a plentiful harvest.

Joanne

October 5, 2005

God Isn't a Sideline Coach

"Batter up!"

"Take a shot!"

"Dunk it!"

I wish I could say as a sideline mom that I've always used sports jargon correctly. I wish I could say that my sideline coaching was crucial to my children's athletic successes. I wish I could say that I was an asset to the team. However, I wasn't the batter who was up, the fielder with the breakaway on the soccer field, or the player with the basketball. I was the mom on the sideline giving directions like I knew what I was talking about.

I'll never forget the time when I realized my children could hear me as I yelled my sideline coaching advice from the bleachers. "Go get it!" I yelled over and over to my son across the soccer field. He was young but could run faster than most of the kids his age. I knew he could get to the ball and score a goal, so I screamed my head off giving this crucial direction. I know he heard me; however, he seemed hesitant to obey me. Seconds later, I noticed every other fan and coach on the sidelines stopped giving directions. "Now he could hear me clearly," I thought to myself. "Eric, go get the ball!" I shouted with my maternal tone of authority.

With his incredible running speed, my son headed to the soccer ball. Wow! He was fast! He loved to run and I loved to watch him. Just as his foot hit the ball and it zoomed towards the other team's goal, the ear-piercing whistle of a referee stopped the play and my cheering.

The silence on the field was deafening. Using some hand gestures, the referee signaled, "Offside."

The other team kicked the ball, and a substitute player replaced my son in the game. Several players from the other team darted the soccer ball around our team, and within moments, they scored the winning goal.

The bleachers emptied quickly and quietly, and I sat there embarrassed and confused. On the drive home from the game, my son explained to me what happened.

"*Offside* means that the ball is behind the players bringing the ball up the field, and we can't touch it until it gets to the halfway mark," he explained.

I felt terrible. "I'm so sorry, honey," I told him. "I didn't understand what was happening. All I saw was that your team could break the tie score if you got the ball and scored." He mumbled a forgiving, "That's okay, Mom," and stayed quiet the rest of the way home.

Two things happened because of this incident. First, I learned to let the coach be the coach and not give directions to my children. Second, my son learned to not listen to directions from anyone but his coach.

How many times do we head in a direction while listening to a voice that sounds like it knows the right way for us but is so very wrong? How many penalties do we pay because we aren't listening to the Head Coach of our lives?

If we think of Jesus as our Head Coach, what does that mean to us?

- He knows all the plays and even the outcome, yet He is our loudest Cheerleader if we listen to Him.
- He lets us play our position using our talents. He loves to see us use our unique talents. It delights Him.
- He sets us up for success. Jesus never gives instructions or directions to us that will lead to our ultimate failure.
- He doesn't expect us to be experts right away, but He gives us instructions and directions throughout the game so we can keep improving.
- He allows for mistakes because He knows we learn the most about making changes in our lives when we do make mistakes.
- He's knows what we are going through because He's an experienced, seasoned Player. Even though He didn't learn by making mistakes, He created the field of life we are in. He knows exactly what the right thing is at all times.

In John 14:23, Jesus tells us: *"If anyone loves me, he will obey my teaching. My Father will love him, and we will come to him and make our home with him."*

Using the soccer jargon, what does that mean? We get to decide to join Jesus' team. When we do, we need to listen to His directions, no matter what. He'll reveal His Instructions to us play-by-play or game-by-game, so we shouldn't expect to have the whole rulebook memorized and live by it right away. As our Head Coach, He'll love us, give us room to exercise our unique talents, help us learn from our mistakes, and set us up for ultimate success in all we do. Being on Jesus' team will be the best thing for us, and even though we may not win every game, we will benefit from just being part of His Team.

But, that verse also covers an incredible benefit to having Jesus as our Head Coach. Think about it: "…*we will come to… and make our home with…*US!" (*capitalization – mine.*) The "we" stands for Jesus, the Father and the Holy Spirit. God comes to us and makes His home with us. In other words, He's always with us on the playing field of life: in the locker room, in the office, in the apartment, in our quiet times and in our not-so-quiet times. Jesus' presence in our hearts is constant. He doesn't quit the team when we don't do what He wants. He doesn't get fired by management or switch to other teams. He's never too busy to practice with us, help us improve our skills, or just be with us after we've made a mistake and need help, understanding, compassion and encouragement. He is our Head Coach and our First Cheerleader.

Let Jesus be your Head Coach today.

If you'd like to know more about the soccer terminology these days, try: http://www.soccer-for-parents.com. I wish there were sites like this back in the days when my children were on team sports. I could have saved them so much bad advice and saved myself so much embarrassment.

Joanne

September 2, 2006

Holiday Nibbles

There's something about the thirty or so days between Thanksgiving and Christmas. They are almost always loaded with more fat, calories, butter and sugar than any other time of the year. It's difficult to go Christmas shopping for others and not be tempted to pick up a pair or two of roomier jeans for myself while I'm out. After all, shopping doesn't always mean I burn off the mountain-sized caloric intake of all the Christmas cookies and bread, lunches out during the frequent shopping excursion, or even the tasty snack samples in the stores while I push my already too heavy cart down the aisles. If I'm not careful, I can nibble myself into the New Year with a lot more need for a January diet plan.

If one cookie can lead to another, can one bible verse lead to another?

Can I nibble my way into a feast on the Word of God or do I starve myself with tiny morsels of truth in between my extended episodes of busyness? Do I take time to sit at the banquet table my Lord has laid out for me, with plenty of life-changing treats throughout the nourishing meal? Do I push away from His Table with just a nibble in my heart instead of a fully satisfied soul enriched by time alone with my Lord?

I've been working through two bible studies this fall. One of them started on a break right before Thanksgiving, and the other one takes a break starting next week. I keep thinking how much more I need the consistency and the accountability of these studies to keep me in the Word through the holidays.

When traditions, expectations and even disillusionments can distract me from the real meaning of Christmas, how can I stay energized by His Word?

Just like eating the cookies, I guess. I can't have just one...
bible verse.

Joanne

December 5, 2006

Passing on H.O.P.E to Others

Recently we shared a special time with our grandchildren at an indoor amusement arcade. It was a joy to watch our 8-year-old grandson Shaun and our 7-year-old granddaughter Alexis just play. One of the indoor activities was a climbing wall, where people strap themselves into harnesses with bungee cords, and then climb a vertical wall as high as they can go. My grandson was eager for the challenge. He loves to climb, and even though he's a little short for his age, he didn't let anything stop him. As soon as the attendant strapped the harness on him, he was up on the wall and climbing.

He made it up half the wall height very quickly. I was amazed at his speed. The footholds sticking out from the wall were closer together at the bottom, but at higher levels, the foot-holds were spaced farther apart. Shaun tried to make his own footholds in the crevices of the simulated rock. Suddenly, he was airborne with only the spring of the bungee cord holding him. He swirled to the ground and held his chest dramatically as he breathed relief. He looked at me with big surprised eyes and admitted out loud, "That scared me."

With barely a moment on the ground, Shaun started up the wall again. It surprised me how little rest he gave himself. He scrambled up the wall in a different direction this time, trying to get away from the spot where he lost his foothold. Again, he swung around loosely to the ground, but quickly restarted his ascent. When his time on the climbing wall was over, he was breathless from his many attempts to get higher. I wonder what it will be like to watch him climb the wall when he is taller and stronger in a few years. I'm sure he'll be ready to climb again soon, no matter what the obstacles are for him.

1 Peter 3:15 says: *"Be ready at all times to answer anyone who asks you to explain the hope you have in you, but do it with gentleness and respect."*

As I pray for my grandchildren daily, I hope some day Shaun and Alexis will ask me about the hope I have in me because of Jesus. Webster's New World Dictionary defines *hope* as, "a feeling that what is wanted will happen." I pray that some day they will want what Jesus gives all of us who ask.

Will I be ready to answer them? How will I answer them? I realize the answer is in the acronym for the word H.O.P.E.

H – Help. We all need help. I need help. You need help. Jesus gives us the help we need. We aren't meant to be alone or have all the answers. We need help. Admitting we need help is the start of knowing Jesus as your help. (Hebrews 13:6)

O – Over. Overcome, overpower, overturn, overpass – with Jesus the worst can be over today. What problem, situation, or circumstance do you trust Jesus to help you overcome today? Whatever it is, He can do it!

P – Pain. We all experience pain in some form or another. Whether it's a scratch needing a bandage or a deep wound requiring surgery, we all have pain. When we remember that everyone has pain, it makes it easier for us to be gentle and respectful. Jesus sees us through the pain.

E – Eternally. Endlessly. Continuously. Perpetually. Jesus never quits, never gives up on us, and never ends His Love for us.

Are you ready to answer anyone who asks you to explain the hope you have in you? It's more than a feeling or a concept. It's the very definition of HOPE.

"So say with confidence, "The Lord is my helper; I will not be afraid. What can man do to me?"
– Hebrews 13:6

"The LORD delivers him in times of trouble."
– Psalm 41:1-2

"In all things we are more than conquerors through Him who loved us."
– Romans 8:37

"For the LORD is good and his love endures forever; his faithfulness continues through all generations."
– Psalm 100:5

June 28, 2006

A Mother Shares it All

Last night, my husband and I drove past the old baseball field. It was filled with three-foot tall children wearing oversized ball caps on their heads and unblemished gloves on their hands. Dads were kneeling on the pitchers' mounds, and Moms where cheering from the sidelines.

It was definitely a flashback moment for me. My boys are in college now, but I remember the tension in the car before each game. For my elder son, it always seemed more intense.

"Do you have your glove?"

"Do you have your water bottle?"

"What time does the game start?"

"Do you see your coach?"

The child burst from the car door in the nick of time, while I found a parking spot and lugged the lawn chair, the snack bag, my purse and as much as I could carry to get to a place on the sidelines to watch my son.

"Mom, coach says I can be the pitcher tonight!"

"That's great, honey. Have fun."

My son always looked tall for his age, until he stood next to a grown man on the pitching mound. Then, he looked so small. Pitching for him at this level meant standing next to the coach of the other team who was throwing the ball to his players. What a big deal it was for him to be the pitcher.

Sharing victories and struggles is part of being a mom.

A few years later, I was the mom on the sideline of the baseball field with tension that lasted the whole game. My son took the mound as the pitcher. He'd practiced pitching for hours on the side of the house. How I became the "side yard" coach for pitching, I don't know. But there I was, crouched down with my glove guarding my face catching my son's pitches as he practiced.

Sharing hopes and dreams is part of being a mom, too.

His team won the first game he pitched. He was ecstatic. I was, too. I wonder if he'll ever know what it meant to me to share with him what he was going through at the time. If he won every game he pitched, that would be one thing. But he didn't. So we have other memories besides winning we share. We both grew a lot through those times.

Sharing the challenges and disappointments is even part of being a mom.

He's in college now. He doesn't have time for sports anymore. He's holding down a job, trying to get through chemistry and calculus, and managing a serious relationship with his girlfriend. He plans to be an engineer, and somewhere in his future, he wants to write a book, continue to write songs and play his guitar, be a father and help others know what Jesus did for him.

Sharing the plans and life purposes is one of the best parts of being a mom.

With Easter just a few weeks ago and Mother's Day just a few days ahead, I've been thinking about the connection. The Bible records that Jesus' mother was there for His first breath and His last breath. As moms, we can empathize with her pain and loss. But she was also there for His Resurrection. Can you imagine the joy in her heart when she found out He was alive again?

Sharing the Resurrection is the absolute best part of being a mom.

If you haven't told your children – no matter what stage of life they are in – that you are on their team, that you support them and are sharing all the big and little things of life with them, maybe it's time you told them. And if your children don't understand about what the Resurrection means for them personally, help them understand that with Jesus they can and will be more than conquerors.

Joanne

May 6, 2006

Congratulations! You're a Normal Woman!

I was recently at a client's office taking photographs of the staff for their website. Although I am not professionally trained in photography, I have learned a few tips and tricks to helping my subjects pose comfortably for the camera. One of the first things I do is listen to what each person says about how they feel about being photographed. This day was no different.

"I never like any photos of me," one woman warned me.

"I didn't have any warning, so my hair is not right," another woman let me know.

"Which jacket should I put on?"

"My eyes close when the camera flashes."

"I'm always the one taking pictures so I don't have to be in them."

The complaints were multiple.

As the last woman took her place before the camera, and I restated my typical adjustments for posing, her lists were just as long as the other women I photographed. I blurted out my clearest observation to her. The rest of the office broke out in laughter.

"Congratulations! You're a normal woman."

There are very few, if any, women I know who love to have their photograph taken. It's almost as bad as asking each woman to stand on the scale in front of a news camera.

Taking a photograph of a woman brings out every hint of perfectionism she has, but most importantly, it brings out every whisper of criticism she's ever heard.

I wonder what God thinks when we criticize our appearance, His creation.

One of the books I've been reading lately by Karon Phillips Goodman has a great title: Grab a Broom, Lord...There's Dust Everywhere! The tagline for the book is "The Imperfect Woman's Guide to God's Grace." Great title! Great book! Important lessons!

Some of the principles she brings out are very memorable. Here's just a quick list of principles from the first 2 chapters:

1. The Lord stands ready to help us with our imperfections because He understands them so well. He created us imperfect. Our imperfections don't have to stop us from enjoying the amazing life He's given us and from doing what we were born to do. He's got them covered.
2. He's not surprised by our imperfections. In fact, it's not perfection from us that God expects, but trust and growth and discipleship – asking for His unique help.
3. God wants us to depend on Him not impress Him with our lack of need.
4. Weak doesn't equal worthless to God. He's not bothered with what we are lacking because we don't have to be perfect to do our work for Him, only committed and willing.

Second Corinthians 3:5 says: *Not that we are sufficient of ourselves to think of anything as being from ourselves, but our sufficiency is from God.* (King James Version)

The author asks some great questions at the end of each chapter in a section she calls, "Looking through the dust…" Maybe it's time you answer them, too.

- In what areas of your life do you obsess about being perfect? How do you feel when you can't be perfect?
- Can you say, "don't be so hard on yourself" to others far more easily than to yourself? What's the difference?
- Do others recognize your need for perfection? How do you explain it to them? To God?
- What work have you neglected or postponed because you felt too imperfect to do it? What would be a better step in your journey with God?

This I Pray…

Lord, in Your grace, please help me past this obsession with my imperfections, and help me accept them instead and show them to You.

The book is colorful, easy to read, and quite insightful. Of course, I did notice that the author's photograph wasn't on the back cover, so she is also a normal woman just like us!

Joanne
November 10, 2006

Single Mom Tears

The door closes. Immediately, the silence slices through the echoes of the goodbyes. The weight of two days alone load down the young mother's spirits. This is the first of many silent weekends she must endure. The strain is almost unbearable already, and it's only been a few seconds since her children left with their father.

There is no stopping them. The tears stream down her already crimson cheeks. Her eyes sting as the intense saline floods every lash. Every pore of her face sloshes with moisture as she throws herself face down onto the second-hand sofa and shudders in her pillow-smothering wailing. Today, she unconsciously decides, she won't force herself to stop the tears. She knows she has nothing left to barricade them now. She has nothing left but tears.

A few hours later, the tornado of emotions subsides for the young woman. The crisp morning sunlight through the window over the sofa is now dull with the passage of time. Shadows dance around the room. Her body aches from the release of her inner turmoil. The silence still stabs at her callously.

"Will I cry like this every weekend?" she asks herself, turning over on the sofa and glaring at the cracks in the unfamiliar ceiling of her new apartment. "Will I always feel this alone?"

She stands unsteadily, dizzy from the hours of being horizontal. She makes it to the tiny bathroom to wash her face and blow her nose on the generic brand tissues. Her throat feels dry and parched from the outpouring of fluids, but nothing quenches her.

The door to the boys' bedroom whispers to her alluringly. It calls to her mother's heart, just as if the boys themselves were on the other side, repeating the impatient "Mom, Mom, Mom" stalling techniques of their nightly bedtime ritual.

She opens the door to an explosion of mayhem. In their hurry, the boys left their room a mess. Shoes, clothes, toys and books are scattered across the shag carpeting. She isn't angry that they didn't do what she asked. It gives her something to do now. Each toy is gently replaced in the toy chest, and each garment is relegated to the hamper. Shoes are paired in the bottom of the closet. The stacks of books, all well worn from the frequent "Read me this one, Mommy" pleas are one by one put on the shelf.

As her chore of love finishes, the young mother turns to the bunk beds and habitually straightens and smoothes the covers. Under the pillow of the lower bunk is her younger son's favorite book: <u>All You Ever Need</u> by Max Lucado. How many times she has read this book to her boys! She stares at the cover illustration, soaking up the gentle smile of the woman pouring water from a heavy jug into a wooden bucket.

"Will I ever smile like that again?" she thinks, as her mind wanders back to her heartache again. Her feelings scroll quickly through her thoughts: "I'm afraid. I'm sad. I'm lonely. I'm tired. I'm lost. I'm worried. I'm needy. I'm so weak. I'm just a mess." No wonder she can't smile anymore. No wonder she aches from the top of her head to the bottom of her feet, and she feels nothing but pain and loss.

She opens the book as she flops to the floor like a discarded teddy bear kicked out from under the covers. The introduction pages are new to her, though, since her children always insisted on jumping straight to the story. The words that stand out to her are, "God's grace is a gift more precious than water in a desert. It is all you and your children ever need."

"God's grace…it is all you and your children ever need." Her mind repeats the principle over and over.

"Even now, God?" her voice breaks the silence for the first time since she stopped crying. "Is your grace really all I will ever need? Is it all the boys will ever need?"

Then, like the warmth of her children's hugs, she feels a glimmer of peace. The truth is clear. Grace is all she needs to get through the silence, to get through the rest of her weekend and all the ones to follow. And, even to get through the rest of her life.

…"*My grace is sufficient for you, for my power is made perfect in weakness.*"…
– 2 Corinthians 12:9

Joanne

October 24, 2004

Practicing the Presence of God

Since I have turned my life and my heart over to God as a twenty-eight-year-old adult, I realize I had missed out on a lot of very important principles about growing closer to God while I was still a child. So, even though it's been almost 16 years, I am trying to catch up on all that I missed.

One huge principle of faith that I needed to learn was practicing the presence of God in my life. What does that mean? For me, it means turning off my "I'll do it on my own" switch in my head to the "I am His" switch, and just dwelling on that truth mentally. It was very difficult for me to do until someone taught me about visualizing in my prayer time. Now, since I am such a visual person, this technique suits me perfectly. It's not a trance-like state or anything hokey. It's just time when I clear my mind from the things I'm thinking about and focus on a scene in my head that brings me closer to God.

Since Father's Day occurs this month, I thought I'd share the visualization I've used for the past few years. It settles me down, reminds me of how much my heavenly Father loves me personally, and gives me such hope for what heaven is going to be like.

I close my eyes and remember a time when I was a little girl, maybe 6 or 7 years old. I picture myself in this huge, grassy field. Everything is bright and colorful. I imagine the smell of the honeysuckle bushes and hear the gentle wind making the grass wave softly ahead of me. The breeze is blowing in my face, and the sun is bright and warm. My arms are sleeveless so I can move around freely, and I begin to swirl in a dance of joy through the field. I'm happy. I'm content.

All I see around me is green and fresh. The trees that line the field are also dancing with me in the breeze, and the birds join with the current to create the melody and rhythm of our movements.

Joining the choreography, a few butterflies appear and flutter along side me. They are yellow and orange, and seem tirelessly excited to touch as many blades of grass as possible.

I spend a long time in this part of the visualization sometimes, because it can take me a while mentally to detach from the whirlwind of my life and focus on the gentle breezes of God's creation instead.

From a distance, I can hear a voice calling my name. It's subtle at first and can barely be heard over my waltzing steps through the grass. When I finally can hear the voice, it stirs me. This is the voice I've always longed to hear – and it's calling my name! I am thrilled completely. I am urged to follow the voice and beginning running in its direction. "Could it be Him?" I ask myself as I rush in the voice's direction. As He calls my name again, I am assured it is He. It is my Father. It is my Creator. It is the same voice that Adam and Eve heard calling their names in the Garden of Eden.

As I am running towards the Voice, I can tell that the Voice is running towards me. I question what I hear. "Can He be as eager to be with me as I am to be with Him?" And, then I hear His Voice answer my thoughts. "I love you, Joanne. I've missed you."

There are times when I vary the end of my visualization. Sometimes, when I find Him, I picture myself folded up in His arms with my head against his chest. Then, I can finally let go of whatever hurt or pain has been keeping me away from Him. His hand always gently wipes my tears and something about His very nature helps me to smile again.

Sometimes, when I find Him, I gush with an explosion of all the words and feelings I've held inside with no one having time to listen to me. I picture His eyes smiling at me, listening intently and hearing every word and every emotion in my heart. Then, there are times when I find Him and I have no words. I have just the deepest sense of peace to just be with Him, and together we walk hand-in-hand around the grassy field, enjoying the warm breeze and the playful butterflies.

Somewhere in this visualization, I grow up from a little girl spending time with her Daddy to a grown woman who still wants to spend time with her Heavenly Daddy.

"Be still, and know that I am God; I will be exalted among the nations, I will be exalted in the earth."
– Psalm 46:10

Joanne
June 10, 2006

Inch by Inch –
For a Purpose

Inch by inch, the trees of the forest rooted themselves deeper into the rich, black soil. Five trees stood close to each other near the middle of the forest. Their earliest memories were a child's hands firming the dirt around their thin sapling stems when they were planted during an Arbor Day scouting activity.

But that was many, many years ago.

Now, the five trees were tall and mighty. They had grown thick with time; their bark chiseled deep lines of identifiable character in each of them. The one tree closest to the small clearing grew the tallest. It was first to be drenched by the rain during the spring showers. It hoarded the sun light and shaded the other trees from the vital rays. The tree farthest from the clearing was the darkest, with its gray-black bark thicker than the others to shield it from the bitter cold of winter. The three trees in the middle competed against each other for attention, producing grand colors in the fall and wrapping their roots around each other to absorb each other's nutrients from the soil and water.

One fall day when all the trees where showing off their best colors, they heard steps tromping in their direction. Two figures stopped between the five trees and looked up.

"When I was a boy scout, I planted these trees," the man said to his son. "Our pack planted over a hundred trees that day, but I got to plant these five."

The trees rustled themselves with pride to stimulate more admiration from their spectators. The towering trees barely noticed the tiny sapling in the boy's hands until he knelt to plant it in the middle of the five trees.

The boy's tiny hands pressed the dirt around the sapling stem, and the mighty trees held the air as still as possible to hear the boy's small voice.

"It was her favorite kind of tree," the boy said. "I hope she can see it from heaven."

The first watering of this tree sapling came from the tears of its planter. Streams of liquid drenched down the boy's cheeks to fall on the newly packed soil around the stem. The father held his son tightly afterward and reassured him that both his mother and God could see the love in the tree and the love in his heart. The two left as silently as they came, with only the tromping of their boots growing softer with the distance.

The five trees couldn't ignore the new addition to the forest. It made them wonder what was going on in the heart of the child who planted them. How did he remember this exact spot? Were they planted with such love? Why did the father bring the boy back to this spot so many years later to plant this little, scrawny twig of a tree?

As time went by, the five trees tended to the needs of their new addition. The largest tree opened windows of light onto the sapling, warming it with the sun and directing rainwater to stream in its direction. The middle trees sheltered the sapling's roots by covering it with their warm, colorful leaves in the fall. Even the darkest tree protected the sapling by hiding it from forest creatures looking for low brush to eat.

Every fall, the trees awaited their visitors. While the father shook his head in disbelief that his own boyhood trees were so tall and mighty, the son measured the height of his own sapling against his own growing stature. They didn't seem to care how different the new sapling looked from the other trees.

One fall, the father and son cheered with delight that the young tree was now bearing fruit. They returned with a basket. Bright red apples filled the basket and the boy's heart with a fond memory of his mother.

"She loved apple pie," the boy's deepening voice said. His father smiled and helped his teenage son gather the fruit. It was time for a deeper lesson than remembering their loved one.

"This tree took patience, time, lots of sunlight and water, and even the shelter and supports of these other trees to help it grow into a mature, fruit-bearing tree," explained the father.

"It is kind of cool that God used the trees you planted when you were a kid to help my tree grow, huh?" the teenager pointed out.

"God uses EVERYTHING for His purpose, son" the father answered, "especially us."

Joanne

December 6, 2005

Put Downs and Pick Ups

I recently spent three days at a women's retreat. The hectic pace I had to work for weeks ahead of the event was exhausting. I worked nearly every night after dinner, and my thoughts of deadlines and pleasing customers tangled my muscles with tension. "All of this for a day and a half off work," was my silent grumble. "Do self-employed people really have the time or the energy to go on retreats?" I shut my thoughts up and tried to concentrate on getting my work done. "It will all be over soon enough," I told myself.

Today is the day after the retreat. My mind won't focus back on work now. It is swirling with exciting memories of closeness with my Savior during worship and treasured moments of honesty with my new friends from the retreat. The taste of daily communion is fresh in my mouth. How I love those sacramental flashes of remembering what Jesus did for me on the Cross and celebrating what He did for me in the Resurrection. There is so much about that retreat I don't want to be over now.

In the sixteen years since I accepted my relationship with Jesus and let Him start changing and growing me as a believer, I've been on dozens of organized retreats. Each one has their own characteristics and prominence in my life. Although some were more about growing closer to people than about growing closer to our Lord, I learned to put down something and pick up something else from each one. This retreat had its own special list of **"Put Downs"** and **"Pick Ups"** for me to change in my life.

- **Put down** busyness, and **pick up** more time alone with the Lord.
- **Put down** procrastination, and **pick up** intentional commitments of my time and talents.
- **Put down** negative attitudes, and **pick up** positive expectations of God's work around me.
- **Put down** what I think God wants me to do, and **pick up** letting Him show me what He wants me to do.
- **Put down** trying to please people, and **pick up** that I am already pleasing to God because of Jesus.
- **Put down** my inability to be sinless on my own strength, and **pick up** that Jesus helps me overcome my sins and all my shortcomings.
- **Put down** my awareness of my own problems, and **pick up** that Jesus can and will make me an over-comer of all my problems.

I'm sure the list will get longer as I fully digest my retreat experience, and the Lord continues to show me why He wanted my focused attention for the three days. I pray that this time, the important principles God wants me to learn will not just stay in my notebook but actually get applied to my heart and life. But, by now, I understand that the process of putting down things and picking up new things is a lifelong activity of faith building. It's not about how much I think I need to get out of a retreat; it is about letting the Lord use it to change me little by little to be more of whom He wants me to be.

For those of you who have been on a retreat or had a significant event in your faith journey recently, I challenge you to ask God to help you make your own **"Put Down and Pick Up"** list of principles. It shouldn't take very long, but the results could last an eternity. It's one way I've learned to not let a retreat really end.

In fact, as I look back on the sixteen years of my faith journey, it is every time I am alone with God, in worship, in Bible study, in relationships and in my quiet time, the Lord is showing me different things to put down in my life so I can pick something else up that He wants for me. So, even if you haven't been on an organized retreat lately, I challenge you to ask God to show you what He wants you to **"Put Down and Pick Up"** for Him. He has something new for you every day.

"*Therefore, if anyone is in Christ, he is a new creation; the old has gone, the new has come!*"

– *2 Corinthians 5:17*

Joanne

October 9, 2006

Regaining my Tools

It was an ordinary moment but a life-changing memory for me. Just a few weeks after I accepted Jesus as my personal Savior, I walked into a Christian bookstore to familiarize myself with the tools of a believer. I was a single mom on a tight budget, however, so there was little I could afford in the store. I found a <u>Bible Promises</u> book on the clearance table for $2 and headed to the checkout counter. There, next to the register, was a *Psalty the Singing Songbook* audio cassette. It only had six songs on it, so it was also bargain priced. I snatched it up and walked out of the bookstore with my $5 purchase and some of the most powerful faith-building tools of my life.

I absorbed the <u>Bible Promises</u> book as fast as I could. I needed the connection with Jesus through His Word deeply, but because I didn't own an easy-to-understand Bible, this tiny book became the lifeline for me learning to look to the Lord for guidance and hope.

When I felt afraid, there were verses of peace I read and reread.

"For I am the Lord, your God, who takes hold of your right hand and says to you, do not fear; I will help you."
– Isaiah 41:13

"So we say with confidence, "The Lord is my helper; I will not be afraid. What can man do to me?"

– Hebrews 13:6

Okay. I read the fear passages a lot. My $2 book didn't look new for very long. Thanks to this tiny, pocket-sized book, I began to receive a mountain-sized faith that carries me to this day.

But it was the moment when I first played the *Psalty the Singing Songbook* tape with my children in the backseat of my small car that was life changing. I ached for the pain I saw on my own children's faces because of the divorce and turmoil in our lives. I love them so much more than I could ever express, and I was eager to share my faith with them. My boys were 4 and 3 at the time, and they had never heard any of these *Psalty* songs before that moment. As soon as the first song came on the cassette, they both immediately started singing along. It was the most incredible sound I have ever heard. My Eric and my Adam boisterously sang along as though it was a song I had sung to them from birth. I never knew the song let alone the principles they were singing. *"God has a plan for my life…"* On so many levels, God comforted me with this timeless truth coming from the mouths of my own children. God does have a plan for their lives.

As if the tape was still in the player and I had pushed the fast-forward button, our lives have fast-forwarded to 2007. Eric is 21 now, and Adam will be 20 in a little over a month. Both are in college and the busyness of life, college, and other priorities distance us much farther than the backseat of that small car. They are on the verge of huge, life-changing decisions now themselves. What direction should they take their careers?

What college will be best for their specialized fields? Who shall they marry? What adventures lay ahead of them? What lies behind them that they need to give to God and move on? I ache all over again for the expressions of stress and pressure I see on their faces now.

Is that my old fear issue coming back up? It's back to the Bible Promises book for me.

"Have no fear of sudden disaster or of the ruin that overtakes the wicked, for the Lord will be your confidence and will keep your foot from being snared."
– Proverbs 3:25-26

"Peace I leave with you; my peace I give you. I do not give to you as the world gives. Do not let your hearts be troubled and do not be afraid."
– John 14:27

Back to my memory of their small, young voices singing from the backseat the truth that "God has a plan" for their lives and that they'll work it out together with Him.

When I look back to the principle of that song, I know where it comes from in the Bible.

"For I know the plans I have for you,"
declares the LORD, " plans to prosper you
and not to harm you, plans to give you hope
and a future."
– Jeremiah 29:11

And, yes, this verse is replayed often in my mind through the voices of my children when they were young. God has a plan for their lives – and for mine.

Joanne

January 11, 2007

Sand in my Sandals

Spring means unburying the sandals from the back of my closet, giving myself a pedicure, and setting out to greet the warmth of summer without socks and shoes. How nice. How relaxing and unwinding. What a pleasant change from the winter months of keeping my toes warm under cotton and leather.

Now that it's after Labor Day, however, I'm ready to lose the sandals and step back into the closed shoe comfort of my other footwear. The needs for changing back are obvious: My feet have an awkward tan line on them now from being exposed to the sun during the summer without me remembering to slather SPF30 below my ankles. My toes are scuffed and scratched from several uncoordinated moments of tripping, running into things, and dropping things on them. My arches ache for the support of laces and insoles.

Probably the most troublesome thing about wearing sandals during the summer for me is the sudden, almost crippling effect of sand when it gets between my feet and the sandals. I'm the first one to admit that I have tender feet. Inevitably, every time I cross a blacktop parking lot, the tiny pieces of gravel magnetically find the sensitive places of my feet. Wincing, I have to stop walking immediately, remove one or both sandals, and wipe off the bottom of my feet before putting the shoes back on. It may be as small as sand in the wrong place, but it is as troublesome as if it were a boulder to me.

Just like my feet are ready for the protection and support of good footwear after Labor Day, I am ready for the protection and support of a good bible study, too. Typically, I participate in a weekly bible study that meets from September to May.

I enjoy the fellowship, but mostly I enjoy the committed structure and accountability to spending time with Lord several times a week to do my lessons at home. During the summer, we don't meet so we can relax with our families, travel and take advantage of the warmer months to get other projects done around our homes. We are supposed to maintain our own quiet time with the Lord, of course, but with so much freedom and so many more things to do, it's hard to keep "God time" in my summer schedule. I can feel the effects now. I realize I've been overexposed to some worldly habits again: like laziness, grumbling, and selfishness. My unguarded mind might be a little bruised and scratched from several inadvertent lapses into temper and negativity. My lack of discipline in studying the Bible means I need to stretch back into a good pattern for my life.

What is interesting to me is that the time I spent during the summer away from my quiet time with God didn't stand out to me like the sand in my sandals. I love Jesus. I am committed to Him. He is my Savior, my Lord and my Best Friend. But, I didn't wince with pain at the realization that I hadn't been alone with Him in days. I didn't stop everything, wipe off what was in the way, and get back to reading the Word and walking straight in His eyes. My heart and my spirit are even more sensitive than my feet are, yet I didn't adjust my life and my schedule when I was so aware of what was wrong in my walk. And, not spending time with God is so much bigger than a grain of sand in my life. It is a mountain of separation for me.

I am so grateful that my relationship with God is unchanging, even when my fellowship with God is distracted by the flexibilities of this world.

The Bible describes it this way:

"This is the message we have heard from him and declare to you: God is light; in him there is no darkness at all. If we claim to have fellowship with him yet walk in the darkness, we lie and do not live by the truth. But if we walk in the light, as he is in the light, we have fellowship with one another, and the blood of Jesus, his Son, purifies us from all sin."
– 1 John 1:5-7.

It is amazing to me the way God immediately meets me on the pages of His Word the moment I start reading the Bible again, no matter how long of a vacation I take from it. Now, back to my bible study…

Joanne
September 9, 2007

Steps to Standing in Faith

What started as an ordinary backache turned into a dramatic new way for me to learn how to stand again. Yes, I was hospitalized in great pain and grateful for the medications that pulsed into my bloodstream to relieve it. In the darkness of my pain, I talked a lot to God. I wondered how our Lord Jesus managed without a morphine drip to dull His dying pain on the Cross. I learned so much about the true love of Jesus and His true sacrifice for me while I felt the most excruciating pain of my life. "Would I go through this for someone else?" I wondered. "Would I go through this for my Lord?" Gratefully, the pain became manageable, and I busied myself with other thoughts.

But it was with my first attempt at getting out of bed that I seemed to learn the most. The nurse assistant who worked on the orthopedic floor broke down the steps for me. I repeated them out loud as I stood for the first time after hurting my back.

- Lift my body with my arms
- Look straight ahead
- Breathe
- Allow for assistance
- Steady myself before taking a step
- Take one step at a time
- Go slow and make each step deliberate

And, as I spoke them, each step revealed a spiritual insight to remember as well:

"Lift my body with my arms," reminds me about the power of God in Exodus 17, during one of the Israelites' crucial battles. It took two men on either side of Moses to hold his arms steady so God's power would win the battle.

This day was a crucial battle for me, and I needed God's power and His strength to steady me. Every battle I am in – whether physical, spiritual or emotional – needs to happen in God's power and strength for me to succeed.

"Look straight ahead" is the key to my posture as well as my hope. Pain changes my focus. I look down, look away, or sometimes even close my eyes when I am in pain. I can't see my progress or where I am going or recognize the new height I am reaching if I don't look straight ahead. I often imagine the posture of the lame man Jesus healed in Mark 2. Without any strength of his own, he looked straight into the face of Jesus and stood. Without any strength of my own, I need to look straight into the face of Jesus to stand through the trials, the hardships and the devastating consequences that affect my life.

"Breathe" is a constant word picture of creation for me. God breathed life into Adam, and with every breath I take, I am re-minded that God is my Creator, my Sustainer and my Source for Life. In the same way focused breathing through childbirth yielded two bundles of joy in my arms years ago, I use the same technique to remember that God breathes life into every person I value. Focusing on His breathing through my pain reminds me that God gives me everything I need to live.

"Allow for assistance" is admittedly difficult for me. But, this step reminds me that God didn't put me on a desert island to fend for myself. Instead, He surrounded me with family and friends who get to carry on His personal love for me through support, encouragement and meeting practical needs. It took faith, courage and persistence of the lame man's friends to carry him to the Lord for healing. It has taken faith, courage and persistence of my husband, my family and my closest friends to carry me to the Lord in prayer every day through this trial. And, yes, many of them have helped me in very practical ways including fixing meals, vacuuming, running errands and countless other mundane tasks that needed to be done.

"Steady myself before taking a step" is a new discipline with powerful results. I didn't realize how hurriedly I ran through my day until I hurt my back and had to start over. I was in the bad habit of bounding to my feet and heading in a direction simultaneously. I guess, spiritually I'd been doing the same thing. I'd say a prayer asking for the Lord's help in a certain area while I was already stepping into the direction I thought I should be taking. It's a deliberate choice to wait now, to pause before heading in a direction after standing to my feet or after kneeling before my Lord.

So now, **"taking one step at a time"** is getting a little easier both physically and spiritually. I realize the first person I need to be patient with is me. My pace for life had to slow up because of my injury, but it also needed to slow up for my spiritual life. I can't rush myself now physically, without wearing out much more quickly and stirring up some kind of new ache or pain in the process. Spiritually, I've realized my hurried up faith also needs the slower pace. I need to take one step at a time in my faith, make sure I'm balanced and on even ground, and stop rushing the paces of my relationship with God and my time with Him.

"Go slow and making each step deliberate" helped me regain my strength for standing, for walking and for healing into a normal, effective life again. I'm back to work, back to the gym and even back to my favorite hobby of traveling with my husband. But, spiritually, I am on new ground. My pace is slower while I focus on His Creation and Power in my life. I take time to breathe Him in more through His Word and my time alone with Him. But, it is my posture that is the most changed. I can look straight ahead with faith. My eyes are focused on the Lord.

Joanne

August 6, 2007

Thanks a Lot

It's more than a parade on TV. It's more than a rare opportunity to pull out the good dishes and check to see if your flatware doesn't have water spots on it. It's more than the volume of household contraptions raising a decibel or two. How many times will I set off the smoke alarm this year?

Yes, Thanksgiving is almost here. I have so much to do, so little time, yet so many things to be thankful for.

Recently, I was driving the minivan while making my mental list of things to do for the holiday. Driving is not a good time to actually write the to-do list, I've learned, so I busied my head with a lengthy "don't forget" list.

- Check in with family members we will be seeing for the holiday.
- Send regrets to the family members we won't be seeing.
- Think through how many seasonings I really need to buy at the grocery.
- Estimate how many back-up jars of gravy I will need in case my attempt at real gravy backfires.

It was a long drive with lots of things on my mind. After I pulled in the garage, I headed straight to my desk to organize my thoughts and write out my extensive list.

And there, sitting in the middle of my desk was mail my husband had sorted for me. A bright yellow envelope was on the top of the stack, and I could hardly wait to open it. It was a Thanksgiving greeting card from my best friend who lives in Michigan.

Immediately, I felt the ache of our long-distance friendship. We are deep spiritual sisters as well, so I cherished knowing the card she picked out for me was genuinely from her heart and filled with details she knew would touch my heart.

Right below her signature was a bible verse that just clicked for me. I've read it a dozen or more times in my life, but how I just needed it now.

"Give thanks to the Lord, for He is good; His love endures forever."
– Psalm 118:1

As much as I have to be thankful for in this world – my family and friends, my health, my business, my ministry, my home and all the needs and wants I have met – I realized I just need to focus on what I really have to be thankful for: God's Love. Of all things I have, God's love is the only thing that is eternal. It will never run out. It will never empty. It will never decline. It will never need a refill or a back-up. It will never end.

Can I ever thank God enough for the way He loves me – with the forever and ever and ever kind of love that only comes from the One who created Love in the first place?

Happy Thanksgiving to you all!

Joanne
November 18, 2006

A Tole Painting Christmas

As the fifth child in a fairly large family, Christmas shopping and giving presents to everyone became quite expensive for me as a kid. Okay, my bargain shopping started early back then. I'll never forget the memory of my mom's best friend, Mrs. Steenrod, taking me to the neighborhood dime store to buy presents for my family one year. I was probably 6 or 7 years old at the time, but she was shocked at the way I stretched my $5 as far as I could to get everyone presents.

Let's see: Johnny could use a hair comb with an insurance company's information on it. That was a dime. And, Kay could use the girly smelling bar of soap for a quarter. Jeanie could use a pen, and Margaret could use the pencil that came with the pen. For Dad, I'm sure he needed another ruler, and Mom needed another dishtowel since I stained one of them. And, of course, MaryAnn really needed another toothbrush, since I had dropped hers in the toilet those few times. Yep. Christmas for 7 people cost me around $1.87. I've always been a bargain hunter, I guess. Mrs. Steenrod seemed to enjoy my creativity.

Several years later, I think I really learned about the gift giving process in another way. My mom gave me a very special gift for my birthday that year: She signed me up for tole painting classes at a nearby craft store. No one in the family ever got to take art classes like that, and I was so excited to really learn how to paint. For Christmas that year, everyone got hand-painted ornaments from me. I spent hours and hours sanding small pieces of wood, finishing them with a light stain, drawing my own design on them, and tediously painting each gift. I spent almost all of the money I earned babysitting on that year's Christmas gifts. I really learned to give that year.

Giving has taken on an even deeper meaning for me now as an adult.

The true meaning of Christmas is so much more than me giving to anyone else. It's not about the price tag or even about the effort I put into the gift. Christmas is about God giving to me. God, the Creator of the Universe, gave me the Most Precious, hand-made outpouring of His love when He came to earth as a baby. Christmas is about receiving more than any of us could give to anyone else.

Christmas is about receiving Jesus as my Lord and Savior.

How I pray you know Him, love Him and have received from Him this holiday. It will change everything,

Joanne

December 9, 2006

Reactions to a Full Hamper

It's that time again. The hamper is full and I'm supposed to do something about it. When my children were little, my reactions to full hampers were much more dramatic. "But you only had this shirt on for 5 minutes!!! Why is it already in the hamper?" Wrinkles, wrong colors, too tight, too big – there seemed to always be some reason of justification in their eyes and irritation in my voice.

Now, I have just one full hamper: the one I share with my husband. Over half of these dirty clothes are mine. I'm not sure I want to count the garments I put in there that were too wrinkled, the wrong color, or too tight. (I can assure you, there is nothing I own that is too big for me.)

I still feel irritated that this is an endless job: carrying the hamper downstairs, sorting it according to color and fabric weight (so that I don't have to iron), and laundering each pile. The image of Jesus' multiplying the loaves and fish to feed 5,000 people comes to mind as I recognize the multiplication of socks that don't match and shirts that swell the piles of clothes across the laundry room floor. Maybe I'm still a little dramatic about the whole laundry thing.

And, then, I remember that I love my husband. I love my kids. I can meet a very practical need for them. When Jesus fed the 5,000 in the passage in Matthew 15:32-38, He met a very practical need. They were hungry. He fed them. Matthew describes Jesus' motivation:

Jesus called his disciples to him and said, "I have compassion for these people; they have already been with me three days and have nothing to eat. I do not want to send them away hungry, or they may collapse on the way."
– Matthew 15:32

"I have compassion for these people," Jesus says. What an understatement! Look what He did for them on the Cross, not just on the mountainside that day. No shortcuts. No easier way. No complaints. No irritations. No excuses. Jesus knew from the beginning of creation that people would need His ultimate sacrifice to be clean once and for all. He carried our "full hamper of sins" to the Cross and didn't leave one sin unwashed.

God invites each of us to come to the Cross. Have we taken our "full hamper of sins" to Jesus today? I am thankful for the hamper and the care that it represents. Responding to Christ is as simple as realizing we have some "dirty laundry" in our lives that needs to be cleaned by Him. We carry sins to Him through prayer in a pile or one by one. He doesn't care about the wrinkles, the colors, or the sizes of sins in the hamper. He's listening. He's not irritated with us or looking for justification. He has compassion for us. He loves us. And when Jesus does our "full hamper of sins," we are permanently laundered.

Joanne
November 8, 2007

Authenticity before the Elliptical Machine

The first time I used an elliptical machine – a popular piece of cardio equipment in most fitness centers – I nearly passed out. I'd never exerted that much so quickly in my life. Within the first 2 minutes, my heart rate jumped to over 180 beats per minute, and I became dizzy to the point of nausea. It didn't help that I was the oldest person in a required gym class for a community college, and it definitely didn't help that my instructor was half my age. I'm not sure what he expected - watching me stumble off the equipment, unable to speak from the intense breathing I was doing; then watching me turn patriotic shades of red, then white, then blue. It was a memorable moment for us both.

After I regained my color and my composure, the nice young instructor asked me some questions about the way I was using the equipment.

"Did you enter in your age?" he asked.

Enter it where, I thought. It's on my driver's license.

"Did you enter your weight in here?" he questioned me as he gestured towards the mission control panel on the contraption.

Gosh, even my driver's license doesn't have the right number for my weight on it, I admitted only to myself. Fortunately, my silence was attributed to my exhaustion from overworking myself more than to my own inner stubbornness to publicizing my personal data, even to a machine.

The next class time, I timidly considered trying the elliptical beast again. After all, it was supposed to be good for my aging knees and feet. I did sign up for the class so that I could learn how to work fitness equipment and lose a few pounds. My frugal brain reminded me that taking this class was cheaper than paying a personal trainer to watch me sweat. Maybe I could make it for 3 minutes before I felt like I might pass out, I hoped.

As I neared the machine, I noticed the young instructor walking towards the same area of the gym as the elliptical machine. Oh, NO! He's going to watch me this time! Panic set in. My heart rate went up even before I put my feet into the flat shoe size plates and grabbed the ski pole handrails. The instructor quickly started pushing buttons on my machine and asked me how old I was to put in the data. How rude! Yes, I know he meant well. Yes, I know he was concerned about my health and my safety. Yes, I know he was a man and such details didn't bother him. No, he didn't know that this was my moment of truth.

I failed miserably.

"Thirty-six," I blurted out, knowing full well that the bottle of drugstore hair color did not take six years off my age. I can't even tell you how badly I lied on the weight question.

For weeks my heart ached that I lied. For weeks my body ached, too, but that was another matter.

"Truthful lips endure forever, but a lying tongue lasts only a moment."
– Proverbs 12:19

There's a lying game I didn't realize I played with God, too. As much as I didn't want that instructor to know my real age and weight, there are things I don't want to reveal to God. Pride was part of that lie, but so was distrust. I expected that young man to remember me because of my weight or my age, not because I was an adult trying to do something I hadn't done before. I was the student who didn't know what to do. I didn't trust him with the truth so that he could show me what to do. Do I trust God with the truth? Do I expect God to judge me when I tell Him the truth, or do I trust God to love me through the truth?

So, now I go to the gym a mile from my house and climb onto the beast twice a week. I enter my real weight and my real age as a real reminder to trust God with the truths in my heart, no matter what they are. For the next thirty minutes, I talk to God from my heart. I practice authenticity before My God and my elliptical machine. Now, that's a workout!

Joanne

December 2008

Lessons from a Squeeze

It was a long five weeks, but he finally made it. He'd battled pain and sickness, daughters and nurses, and even his own weakened condition, but he was finally home. I had the privilege today of driving my 81-year- old father home from a skilled nursing facility after his long hospital stay.

There are moments that mean the world to me as a mother, as a wife, as a friend and as a daughter. Today was the daughter moment I will play over and over in my head for the rest of my life. It was the moment he settled himself in his big, plush recliner just minutes after he arrived home. His eyes welled up with tears, and his face settled with the first real sense of peace in over six weeks. He had made it home.

Just a few weeks ago, I had another daughter moment that haunted me every day. My dad lapsed into respiratory distress following his "no other way" surgery to repair adhesions in his bowel. Ugh. I hate that word. I've used it too much in recent weeks. But it's a necessary organ and a frequent area of distress for my father, especially since his 1991 resection. His respiratory distress called for the painful conversation that all children fear.

"Can you hear me, Dad? Can you squeeze my hand? That's it. Good. Now, we need to know your wishes. Do you want them to put you on a vent? Do you want any extraordinary measures if you stop breathing or your heart stops? Squeeze my hand twice if you do, Dad."

There was only one squeeze.

The vocabulary at times like those is incredibly confusing. What is the difference between a full code and a DNR? What will they do if he stops breathing? Will the forced air oxygen mask, a bi-pap machine, be enough to help him? Does he know what's going on? If they intubate him, will he come off the vent? Is this reversible? Is this his time?

But now, there's this new expression in his eyes. He's resting now. He's done his usual routines of winding the grandfather clock and flipping the channels on the TV remote in his hand. He's chitchatted on the phone with one of the daughters. He's told me where to put his things and reassured me he'd get to his stack of mail tomorrow. He just needs to relax. His fight for life is over.

Now, he gets to live.

I needed to ask a dear friend to help me find the biblical principles from this recent life lesson. I'm honestly still looking for answers to the "Why not?" and "How come?" and "Why us?" questions. Her fresh perspective and extraordinary example to me of devotion to God through the study of His Word instantly gave me focus.

She pointed me to the story in the Bible about the Israelites' reactions to hearing what fight was still ahead of them to get into the Promised Land in Numbers 14. The people grumbled and wept, trembled and complained at what they heard and feared the most. There was "no other way" for the Israelites to experience ultimate peace in the Promised Land until they trusted God. They had a long way to go, but God was going to do the fighting for them.

It's like God was saying: "Can you hear me, child? Can you squeeze my hand? Good. Now, do you know my wishes? Do you know my Will for your life? I want you to breathe into you all my promises of life. I'll do all the extraordinary measures necessary to take care of you and give you eternal life with me. Do you trust me? Squeeze my hand twice if you do."

Do we only squeeze once? Do we never squeeze at all?

Joanne
March 2008

Jelly Bean Transactions

There's a flavor to spring. Did you know it? Sure, spring is bright and colorful with the winter clouds dispersing and the sun warming the ground. It smells incredible with the freshly cut lawns and blooming flowers wafting fragrances around. But I connect spring with taste: the sweet, delicious and tantalizing tastes of candy in my childhood Easter basket.

Even as an adult, I relate spring to candy. There are so many kinds: chocolate Easter bunnies, marshmallow peeps, malted milk balls, solid milk chocolate eggs, Reese's peanut butter cups, Cadbury eggs - plus so much more. By the way, I was very pleased a few years ago when the people at M&Ms started selling pastel pink, blue, green, and yellow M&Ms instead of the primary colors available the rest of year. In my mind, pastel M&Ms taste better, too.

Ah, but the store shelves always fill up with jelly beans this time of year. I also always fill up with jelly beans this time of year. It's my annual obsession that goes back to my childhood. I was the one kid in the family who would trade anything in my Easter basket for everyone else's jelly beans. I really don't know if I ever really liked peeps. To be honest, I never gave them a chance. They were quickly traded to my sister who loved peeps for all the jelly beans in her basket. Then, I would trade my milk chocolate eggs for someone else's jelly beans. To me, Easter Sunday was more about the continuous barrage of "Let's Make A Deal" transactions throughout most of my childhood.

It wasn't until I was much older that I understood about the Ultimate Transaction: the one Jesus did for me on the Cross and in His Resurrection from the dead.

I was 28 years old when I finally understood that I needed Jesus to open the doors to my eternity with Him and open my heart to Him in this life.

Since then, my love for jelly beans is minute compared to my love for Jesus. However, I am grateful that someone ingeniously tied jelly beans to Jesus a few years ago. My sister gave me a small jar filled with yellow, white, black, red and green jelly beans. It was the perfect gift for me, and it reminded me of the Ultimate Transaction when I accepted Jesus.

This illustration is taught in Sunday school classes across the country. It's called the "Gospel According to Jelly Beans."

Yellow Jelly Bean – reminds me of Heaven. The Bible says, *"...God is the light and in him is no darkness at all."* (1 John1:5)

Black Jelly Bean – reminds me of the one thing that cannot be in Heaven: Sin. Sin is inside everyone and it's the part of us that desires to have our own way instead of God's way. *"...for all have sinned and fall short of the glory of God..."* (Romans 3:23). All means every one of us.

Red Jelly Bean - shows the way God made for me to have my sins forgiven, that is, taken away. God loves me. He sent His own Son, the Lord Jesus Christ, from Heaven to take the punishment for my sin (John 3:16), through His Crucifixion and Death on the Cross.

White Jelly Bean - reminds me that we can be made clean from sin by believing the truth about Jesus dying on the Cross for each one of us personally. (I John 1:7). It was a choice for Jesus to die for me personally, and I get to choose to accept His Gift of Forgiveness personally. My sins are gone. I am clean because of Jesus.

Green Jelly Bean - reminds me of my new life received from God. The color green reminds me of things that grow outdoors, like leaves, grass, flowers, and trees. I still have so much to learn about Jesus that I am still growing years later. The Bible says to *"...grow in grace in the knowledge of our Lord and Savior Jesus Christ...."* (II Peter 3:18).

By the way, I kept the jar, but ate the jelly beans. I still have so much to learn.

Joanne

March 2008

Mothering like Mom

I never really felt that Mom and I had much in common. Physically, I am over a foot taller than she. I have green eyes and she had blue. Politically, we were very different. Spiritually, I was distant from God and from my family. Our conversations when I was a younger mom were limited to news about the kids and the neighborhood. When we talked on the phone, it was light and guarded. It wasn't until her later years that I began to see the real resemblance between us.

The first signs of her autoimmune disease took us all by surprise, especially her. As a woman who never whimpered about physical pain, she was suddenly thrust into a world of excruciating torment. The only treatment was a lifelong regiment of prednisone, which had its own nasty side effects to her body.

As she weakened, our relationship strengthened. She allowed me the privilege of helping take care of her, taking her to doctor appointments and even putting her in the hospital for the last night of her life. As I sat there with her alone in her room, I realized she taught me somewhere in my life how to care, how to give and how to mother. In her last hours, she allowed me to mother her. We were always different, but yet we had so much in common.

One of Mom's favorite authors was Erma Bombeck. I remember Mom reading to us from time to time during dinner some passages of Erma's different books. Mother would laugh and laugh while she read. I would scratch my head trying to figure out what was so funny. Then I had my own children. It didn't take long for me to finally get Erma's sense of humor...and my mom's.

I recently found a quote of Erma's that I think could have been said by my mom: *"When I stand before God at the end of my life, I would hope that I would not have a single bit of talent left, and could say, 'I used everything you gave me'."*

I often think of how much my mom gave to her husband, her six children, her grandchildren, and even her great grandchildren. Then there were all her neighbors, her friends, her co-workers and extended family. She really was tireless. She did seem to give everything she had to everyone else.

In that way, I hope I will always be like my mom.

Joanne

May 4, 2008

Respect and Truth

If you've been watching our culture these days, there seem to be more and more people being disrespectful to each other in order to earn respect for themselves. On the tails of the political season with hours of negative ads tainting the media for months at a time, people felt they had the right to disclose every feeling or impression they had about someone else. Yes, people should know the truth. But sadly, when the truth is not reported as much as opinions, and when biases are called facts, it's hard to sort it all out.

So, what does God say about respect? What does God say about the truth? What does God say about integrity? There are 224 passages that use the word truth in the Bible. Even Pontius Pilate asks Jesus "What is truth?" as He stood before Pilate's court confessing the truth that He is the King (John 18:37-38). Obviously, even when the TRUTH is standing right in front of us, we'll deny it.

I am feeling sad today that the biblical understanding of the TRUTH and RESPECT are lost in our culture. We become defensive and aggressive when we offer our opinions as truth and disrespect each other because of our differences.

Jesus gives us this answer:

"I tell you the truth, the Son can do nothing by himself; he can do only what he sees his Father doing, because whatever the Father does the Son also does. For the Father loves the Son and shows him all he does. Yes, to your amazement he will show him even greater things than these. For just as the Father raises the dead and gives them life, even so the Son gives life to whom he is pleased to give it. Moreover, the Father judges no one, but has entrusted all judgment to the Son, that all may honor the Son just as they honor the Father. He who does not honor the Son does not honor the Father, who sent him."

– John 5:19-23

Jesus is the Truth, and all honor and respect is ultimately from the Father. Now that is settled, can we get back to honoring and respecting God?

November 25, 2008

The Channels of Life

I was reading a marketing site yesterday where the resident expert was sharing his research on the generational differences in managing media intake. He said that the number of channels (input of information) that our generation can manage simultaneously is 1.7. For example, on average, most of us can watch TV, read a magazine, and be full aware of both channels of information. Not bad, huh?

He said, however, that the next generation is more capable of handling up to 5 channels of media simultaneously. So, our children can play a video game, text message, surf the net, instant message or chat with someone online, and talk on the telephone and still retain the majority of information. It slowed me down to realize how much more our children and grandchildren will be exposed to just because of the increased capacity of technology.

I'm not sure I could ever manage that many channels of information at once. I think I need music on in the background while I work to tune out other channels of information, so I can concentrate. I listen to about 20 hours of CDs I've bought over the years, all stored on my hard drive and set to play in random order. They range from Christian artists on the WOW Collections to individual artists including: Mercy Me, Newsboys, Michael W. Smith, Stephen Curtis Chapman, Casting Crowns, Mark Shultz and just about any good Christian artists for the last 6 or 7 years.

Anyway, while I work, I listen. This morning, I found a website that has wonderful videos that also tell the messages with visuals. It is called Godtube and the videos just settled my spirit.

So, while I get back into work today, I hope and pray that a little "GodTube" channels its way into your life, and you can be blessed to take in a little more Him while the world is trying to overwhelm you with every other channel in this life.

Joanne

May 14, 2008

A Funny Thing Happened While my Children Grew Up

I'm not sure how it happened, but while my children grew up, I seem to have grown up, too. Somewhere between the "playing patty cake" with my infant son's hands, teaching him to drive donuts in a parking lot before he received his learner's permit, and going over his budget with him before he moved into his own apartment, I grew up.

I remember believing the lie that when I turned 20, I was almost too old to get married, and that I needed to get started in my life. I remember arrogantly telling my parents that I knew everything I needed to make informed decisions: when to get married, when to drop out of college because getting a degree wasn't going to affect my career, how to pick life-long friends, and what to do when problems arise.

Looking back, I can see the love my parents had for me in their eyes. They conversed rationally with me as I emotionally erupted on every point with them. I was determined and head-strong. I believed the lie that I knew what was best for me and that they were trying to hold me back from happiness.

In The Purpose Driven Life, Rick Warren explains that "Spiritual growth is the process of replacing lies with truth." (Warren 2007, 185) Over the past twenty-five plus years, I've experienced the pain of many of the lies I believed, but I've also experienced some unchanging truths that carried me through the brokenness and hardships. The lies were replaced with the truth: God's Truth - sixty-six books worth of truth - the Bible. And with the reality that I definitely didn't know enough then, and still don't know enough now on how to guide my life without God's Truth from the Bible, that has tamed my arrogance.

Maybe being a grown-up means accepting that I am forever a child in the eyes of God and that I've never had to make my own decisions without Him. He's always listened, even when I'm so emotional I'm more like a volcano than a child. He's always cared about the tiniest consequences for my arrogance, stubbornness, and self-misdirection. He's been calmly filling my heart with the truths of His Love, His Character and even His purpose for me while I've been filling my head with lies and misinformation. He's the only one who knows what's best for me.

I now look at my sons with great love and patience. Just like my parents looked at me; just like God does for me every day. Maybe now, I am a grown-up.

Joanne

May 13, 2008

Mimicking the Psalms

"Blessed is the man who does not walk in the counsel of the wicked or stand in the way of sinners or sit in the seat of mockers. But his delight is in the law of the LORD, and on his law he meditates day and night. He is like a tree planted by streams of water, which yields its fruit in season and whose leaf does not wither. Whatever he does prospers. Not so the wicked! They are like chaff that the wind blows away. Therefore the wicked will not stand in the judgment, nor sinners in the assembly of the righteous. For the LORD watches over the way of the righteous, but the way of the wicked will perish."
– Psalm 1:1-6

There are 150 Psalms to read and meditate on in the Bible. Each one has a purpose in the context in which it was written and now in the context of my life. I've been trying to get the "pattern" of the Psalms in my mind, heart and especially my prayer life. There are times, especially when my emotions are huge and my patience level is tiny, that I need to write my own psalms to God in my prayers.

I've noticed that almost all of the Psalms in the Bible have these components:

- Recap - my human situation
- Reframe - from God's perspective
- Rejoice - about God's power and ultimate control

I think that the mistake I often make is that I leave out or rear-range the order of these components. For instance, if I just skip straight to the "rejoice" component, and leave out the "re-cap" element, I still feel distant from God. I need the time to be honest with God, tell Him what I am really thinking and feeling, and trust Him with my human situation. Yes, I know that God knows what's going on, but I need to use my words to describe and communicate with God. It is the "relational" time I have with God: telling Him what's going on and what I am feeling.

"Reframing" my situation from my perspective to God's per-spective is equally important. The God of eternity knows what the outcome of my circumstances will be, and I need to take time trying to view my short-term problems with His long-term results. There are times when my heart hurts so deeply, I can't see my situations from God's view. Suffering, pain, loneliness, loss - these are just a few of my human perspectives that need Godly refocus. This is the hardest component for me. I have to remember God's character as He reveals it to me through the Word and through the work of the Holy Spirit in my heart. Is He trying to grow my character? Is He trying to build my depen-dence on Him? Is He teaching me that He's the only one with perfect love for me?

"Rejoicing" is the culmination of the Psalms and of my life. After I've taken time to relate to God, to share my heart honestly and vulnerably with Him by recapping, and then use all the things I know about God - His Character, my purpose and His plan for me - I can truly rejoice in Him. True rejoicing happens when I take the time and effort to recap and reframe my life. Those previous components help me be more authentic before God in my rejoicing. The more real I am before rejoicing or worshiping God, I've learned then my rejoicing is more true to my heart. I want my life to be a psalm for God.

Joanne

May 3, 2008

Mementos in All Kinds of Shapes & Sizes

"... In the future, when your children ask you, 'What do these stones mean?' tell them that the flow of the Jordan was cut off before the ark of the covenant of the LORD. When it crossed the Jordan, the waters of the Jordan were cut off. These stones are to be a memorial to the people of Israel forever."

— Joshua 4:6-7

I have a large collection of plastic cups in my kitchen. My collection started when my first son moved on from breast milk and bottles to holding his own cup as a toddler. It was always important to me that my children drank plenty of milk, so the only real choices I gave them were about the cup their milk would be poured into. "Do you want your milk in the red cup or the blue one?" *(Note that I rarely asked them if they wanted anything else but milk to drink.)* Each boy adapted to his favorite cups, and life went on with plenty of spilled milk in the process.

Zoom ahead twenty some odd years in time. I still have a bountiful collection of plastic cups in my kitchen. Two whole shelves in the cabinet closest to the refrigerator are their storage and selection display. Some are mementos from restaurants; others are take-homes from trade shows, retreats and school fundraising events. I do have some cups that actually match each other - like they were part of a complete set - but mostly they were used during those "have-to-be-fair-and-give-the-same-amount-to-both" years of parenting. Some of them have barely recognizable logos and images on the sides, while others have indelible stains and scratches from non-milk related activities in the backyard.

The collection of cups is worth little to anyone else but a mom who remembers her grown children's once tiny hands wrapped around them and the simultaneous milk mustaches that occurred. Each silly old plastic cup has a fond memory for me tied to it.

Does God have fond memories stored up of our close times with Him? Does He have mementos about those quiet times while reading His Word that we "spilled the milk" of our problems, insecurities, circumstances and brokenness before Him? Do we still have the "cups" stored in our heart cabinet of times of nourishment and refreshment with God?

I love knowing that God wants us to remember close times with Him in our spiritual lives. From Noah to Revelation, the Bible recounts stories of people building altars to worship God and remembering what He's done in our lives. Stopping to praise God after every battle, after every journey, after every milestone is important. Taking time to remember is important to us and to God.

Joanne

May 1, 2008

Silly Putty in His Hands

When I was a kid, I kept myself busy for hours with Silly Putty - the stretchy, rollable, flesh-colored glop of rubbery plastic sold in brightly colored egg-shaped containers. To be honest, I have no idea what Silly Putty is made from. It could be plastic, or it could be rubber, or it could be over-processed play-doh. Chemistry was never one of my talents. All I know is that I used Silly Putty for many things: modeling clay, snakes, bouncy balls, rings, bracelets, playing catch, masks, darts, and so much more. I think I spent most of the time on Sunday afternoons pressing the Silly Putty onto the comic section of the weekend newspaper, transferring the image onto the flattened ball, and stretching it in every direction until the image wasn't recognizable anymore. Then, I'd start again.

I went to a memorial service last night. A letter written by the relatively young widow was read by one of my good friends. The letter started with the woman's appreciation for all our prayers; then she detailed many specific ways that God's provision was taking care of the family. The letter ended with a challenge to the audience to make our choices count.

Our choices are the modeling clay for our lives.

The illustration Paul uses to depict our status as "clay" is in Romans 9:21. Paul asks, *"Does not the potter have the right to make out of the same lump of clay some pottery for noble purposes and some for common use?"*

Now, the question is, "Am I Silly Putty in God's Hands?"

Do I let Him mold me, stretch me, and transfer His Image onto me over and over again? I Do I let Him stretch me, pull me, kneed me, roll me up then flatten me out on a daily basis?

It is a daily choice - not just on Sunday afternoons with the comic section in front of me.

Joanne

April 29, 2008

When the Bubbles Pop

"So do not throw away your confidence; it will be richly rewarded. You need to persevere so that when you have done the will of God, you will receive what he has promised."
— Hebrews 10:35-36

Devotional:

It's a childish thing to do, but I still love to blow bubbles. I keep a bottle or two of that sticky, soapy, messy stuff with the plastic wand in the kitchen pantry near the back door. I even have a bottle in my minivan for those unplanned stops at the park.

Just like the bubbles drift away as I blow them, my mind drifts away watching them. I study them closely. Each one is a different size but they each reflect the colors of the rainbow. Some pop quickly while others linger and dance in the breeze. Some bubbles leave the wand with several bubble friends, while others start alone and end alone. Depending on how slow or forceful I breathe, I can try to create more or less bubbles at a time. However, I am constantly aware that even though my breath is important to starting a bubble, I have no idea where it will end up or how long it will last. I can only watch and see what happens.

Recently, I received devastating news. The shock and stages of grief are still wafting over me. Instinctively, I pulled out my bottle of bubbles and headed to the park. I was eager for my mind to drift away from my circumstances. The first bubbles were the hardest to blow that day. I barely had breath to exhale through my tears. "Keep trying. Keep blowing," my mind coached me that day. Or, was it God's voice coaching me?

The principles of blowing bubbles seem to apply to so many circumstances in life. "Keep trying. Keep blowing." These words are another way to express the principles of 1 Timothy 4:15-16:

"Be diligent in these matters; give yourself wholly to them, so that everyone may see your progress. Watch your life and doctrine closely. Persevere in them, because if you do, you will save both yourself and your hearers.
– 1 Timothy 4:15-16

I am still trying to see the colors of the rainbow in my situation. God keeps His promises (Gen 9:16) because He loves us with an everlasting love. I realize that no matter how long things last, I get to appreciate them. I get to notice the uniqueness of each person I meet, each friend I have, and each child I raised. I have no idea where any of them will end up, but I am grateful to be part of their "dance in the breeze."

And, when the bubbles of life pop, I get to take another breath and start again.

This I Pray...

Lord, you breathed life into me first and now I pray every breath I have gives you glory and honor. You are the Creator, and all things start and end with You. Give me your eyes to appreciate those around me, your strength to keep going through my circumstances, and your breath of hope to share with others.

Application Steps:

What circumstances in your life does God want you to keep your eyes on what He is doing around you?

Talk to God about the areas in your life where you are struggling to have hope and confidence in Him to work things out as He sees fit.

Simplify your life so you can have time to meet with God through studying the Bible and prayer.

Power Verses:

"Be strong and take heart, all you who hope
in the LORD."
– Psalm 31:24

"But as for me, I will always have hope; I
will praise you more and more. My mouth
will tell of your righteousness, of your
salvation all day long, though I know
not its measure."
– Psalm 71:14-15

"Therefore, if anyone is in Christ, he is a new
creation; the old has gone, the new has come!"
– 2 Corinthians 5:17-18

May 2007

[This devotional was published May, 2007 in Proverbs 31 On-line Devotionals]

Joanne was inspired to write this devotional when she first learned of her cancer. From her personal journal, she writes...

"I am trying to connect to you, LORD. I sat outside on the deck for a while this evening before Margaret came over, and blew bubbles. Sloppy thing to do. Simple thing to do. I am grateful I have the breath to do it now. How sad that lung cancer may mean that some time in the future, I may not be able to breathe efficiently or effectively. Will I be one of those people toting an oxygen tank wherever I go? Will I end up with one of those contraptions like Mother had; tying me to a leash of oxygen line like it did her?

When the Bubbles POP – there's the title for a devotional. Now, how do I paint a picture of hope with that? Keep trying. Keep blowing. Keep an eye out for the film that's on the wand. Sometimes it looks like it's there and sometimes it's not. Take your time. Breathe gently. Breathe slowly. Watch what you start and then watch it float. No matter what you start, you don't know where it will end up. LORD, give me the scriptures you want to tie it all together tomorrow."

With that thought in mind, she wrote this beautiful devotional. It has been published on several websites and magazines.

Afterword

Joanne offered precious time to share her faith journey in her writing. She wanted to set an example of how precious life is and how wonderful it is to read about and become friends with others who are on the journey of life. Joanne's faith helped her every step of the way. She wanted more people to share her journey, have the opportunity to know Jesus in a personal way and she wanted to extend this invitation to people all the time. Will you accept?

Join the Next Step of Faith community. Subscribe to the news-letter. Submit your own writing and vote for your favorites. Encourage women to write about life and faith. Share the book and the website with a friend.

We look forward to meeting you online.

http://next-step-of-faith.com

Notes

Notes

Scriptures

Scriptures

Catalog of Connections

Catalog of Connections

Ideas for Writing My Own Devotional